TIPS FROM THE TOP

book 2

TIPS FROM THE TOP

52 more golf lessons by

the country's leading pros

from SPORTS ILLUSTRATED

compiled by **Herbert Warren Wind**

illustrated by **Anthony Ravielli**

Prentice-Hall, Inc.

Englewood Cliffs, N. J.

Preface

IN 1896, when golf had been played in the United States for less than a decade and was a relatively new vice in England, Willie Park, Jr., a Scot from Musselburgh who had won the British Open in 1887 and 1889, hearkened to the lark of commerce and wrote a very successful and edifying book of instruction entitled "The Game of Golf." The cover of the copy I have—a third edition—depicts an antique golf bag, filled with only two woods and two irons, lying across a rather primitive tee-box. However, as someone or another has remarked, you cannot judge a book by its cover. Here, for example, is a brief excerpt from a passage in which Mr. Park is discussing the overall concept of the swing:

> The club should be swung backwards at a good speed, but without jerking and without undue rapidity, and at the end of the upward swing the downward should be immediately commenced without pause, the downward swing increasing in rapidity until the ball is struck. I believe a great number of faulty styles of golf arise from the fact that there is an effort made to put force into the downward swing from the moment of its commencement. This, I think, is a mistake, as the club should gather speed, and consequently force, as it descends, the greatest amount of force being put into the stroke just before impact with the ball—say, within a foot or two of it.

As this excerpt may serve to indicate, one of the unexpected profits a reader receives from reading Willie Park's golf book—or, for that matter, any good book on any subject written at any time—is a reawakened appreciation of the general hepness of bygone generations. The people who live in every age, it would seem, invariably get so entranced with the theories they are projecting and the techniques they are discovering that apparently it is only a short step to presuming that they and their contemporaries are out-and-out wonders and the folks who went before knew nothing whatsoever and were lucky to find their way to the bakery.

Although Mr. Park's book would not be the ideal guide for the modern golfer in many important respects—it was written when the gutta percha ball and not the rubber-cored ball was being played, and the gutty called for a different manner of attack—his fundamental understanding of how the game should be played is so up to date that it leads one to believe that since the dawn of golf there probably never was a time when certain basic principles were not known, preached, and occasionally practiced. In my mind's eye, for instance, I can see an ancient Scottish golfer standing on the ramparts of Seton Castle one fine day in 1567, looking down on the fields below where Mary, Queen of Scots, is playing a few holes shortly after Darnley's death. "Ah, the Queen wad mack a verra guid gowffer," the Scot muses as he watches, "if only she wad keep her haid doun an' follow through. An' it wad na' hurt Her Majesty either if she wad play the ba' a wee bit fairther forward, jist inside the left heel, like I do masel'."

In his preface to his book, Willie Park, Jr., explains his reasons for writing it: "Although professional golfers have always been teachers of the game, their instruction has been imparted more by example than by precept. Such a method was and is undoubtedly the best, but it is not available to the same extent at the present day as it was, say, fifty or even twenty years ago, and hence a demand has sprung up for books of instruction." I don't think anyone will quarrel with that general premise. Regardless of the quality of an instruction book, it is at best a substitute for person-to-person instruction, and not always a good one. A book cannot take into account the particular capabilities and idiosyncrasies of each player, it cannot tell him where he has fallen into a major error with his hands while he was concentrating on correcting a minor error in his body turn, it cannot tell him what he is doing splendidly, etc.—and all these things a seasoned professional should be able to do for the pupil.

As far as I know, there has been only one man who developed a game of championship calibre simply by reading how-to books, and that man, Walter J. Travis, was such a remarkable cuss that he really shouldn't count. It is an amazing story. An Australian-born perfectionist with more than a touch of Hogan in his makeup, Travis was thirty-five when he decided to take up golf. That was in the autumn of 1896. He collected the books on the game that were considered to be the best and coolly decided that there were two that stood head and shoulders above the others: Horace Hutchinson's disquisitions in the Badminton Library's volume on golf, and our old friend Willie Park, Jr.'s, "The Game

of Golf." He pored over the two books all winter long, swinging, analyzing, and, unusual man that he was, even daring to
modify some of the *do's* and *dont's* he thought were not quite
right for his own individual physical equipment and natural
movements. The following spring, in another manifestation of
his awesome self-discipline, Travis played only three or four
rounds on the course on Long Island he had joined, for he
deemed it more productive to practice his swing and his shots
until he was pretty well along in cultivating what we today
would call his "muscle memory." The next year, 1898, this
aged sophomore in golf entered the United States Amateur and
made his way to the semifinals. In 1900 he won the Amateur.
He won it again in 1901 and 1903, and in 1904—would you believe it!—he took himself over to England and did what no for-
eign player had ever been able to do before: to the infinite consternation of the entire island, Travis carried off the British
Amateur championship. Yes, I think we are best off regarding
this sort of fellow as the exception that proves the rule and letting it go at that.

Although we at *Sports Illustrated* would like to think that
TIPS FROM THE TOP is the clearest and most helpful means
of non-oral instruction ever presented to golfers (largely because Anthony Ravielli has gone far beyond any previous artist
in picturing the exact details and nuances of "feel" intended by
the contributing professionals), there are a couple of points that
the golfer-reader would be wise to keep in mind. First, since
the odds are that he is not Walter Travis reborn, he would do
well to think of the tips as supplemental aids to improving his
game and should continue to regard person-to-person instruction from experienced professionals as primary; in golf the
player himself cannot observe what he is doing and, as the Chi-
nese say, a good pro is worth ten thousand full-length mirrors.
Then, too, the golfer-reader will benefit most from TIPS FROM
THE TOP if he exercises whatever Travisian discipline he happens to possess. Although it will do him no harm whatsoever
to read through all the tips for the pleasure of hearing what the
experts have to say, when it comes to incorporating the tips into
his own game, he should not try to build Rome in a single day.
Rather, he should select one tip, or at the most two, to work on.
When he has digested these two tips fully, then he is in a posi-

tion to work on one or two more with a reasonable expectation of profit. This, of course, is how the finest competitive golfers tune up their games, giving one phase of their swing all of their attention and "mastering" that phase before moving on to another.

One more word of caution: The practice fairway is the best place to experiment with any and all changes. There, with no complicating worries about his score or where the ball is going to end up, a golfer can put all of his mind on executing the actions prescribed by the pros. Let us say, for example, that he knows he has been moving his head all over the place and desires to check his head position à la Harry Cooper. After one or two unhurried sessions on the practice tee, he should be far enough advanced in the cultivation of the right habits so that, when next he plays a round, it should be no trouble at all for him to play his shots with the same correct action he practiced.

Golf takes work if you would play it well, and it takes sense to know how and when to work on it and when to leave it alone. I think we cannot do better than to return to Willie Park, Jr., for a short summing-up on this subject:

> Golf is a fickle game, and must be wooed to be won. No good can be got by forcing the game; and unless one feels fit and has a keen interest in the match, it is better not to play. It is no use going out and playing a round in a half-hearted, listless, indifferent way. Playing in this way is ruinous to good golf; and whenever one loses interest in the game, he is better to stop playing until he feels he can throw his mind and his heart into it. There is no greater mistake than playing till one becomes stale. Further, golf is a business-like game, and should be gone about in a brisk, business-like way. It is far better to play and walk around the links smartly and quickly than to creep around at a snail-like pace. Therefore choose a partner who will not keep you back by slow play. It is impossible to play good golf if you are thinking of something else all the time, and if you have any business worries, leave them behind when you go to the links.

Aye, and the reverse.

HERBERT WARREN WIND

Table of Contents

TIPS FROM THE TOP

1 | TIP FROM THE TOP

from **JOHN BATTINI**
Olympic Country Club,
San Francisco, Calif.

Wrist Putting

EVERY GOLFER has his own special style of putting. I have used my style for thirty years now and I intend to continue with it, even though many people tell me it isn't "modern." This modern style they refer to is the very upright, firm-grip, no-wrist method which many of our tournament pros employ today and achieve their wonders with.

If I seem to contradict this style (in which the stroke originates in the shoulders), so be it. As the saying goes, the answer for each golfer is at the bottom of the cup. I find I putt best by using a very light, very delicate grip that requires about the same pressure I would apply to the wheel of an auto equipped with power steering. I use wrist break. The wrist is the hinge of my stroke, and you might compare this wrist action to the consistent swinging of a garden gate. After taking the club back, I hesitate an instant before beginning the forward stroke. I use plenty of follow-through, exaggerating that action.

My experience leads me to believe that the average golfer—the man who has neither the time nor the talent to master a somewhat unnatural, if efficient, style like the upright—will do very well on the greens sticking with an old-fashioned method such as I have described. He will "feel" the ball better on the putter head.

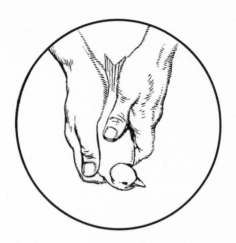

Grip the club almost as if you were holding a small bird in your two hands

The backswing

The follow-through

TIP FROM THE TOP

from **BILL ZONKER**
Seattle Golf Club, Seattle, Wash.

Inside the Barrel

ALTHOUGH most golfers certainly understand that the body supplies the motive power that their hands actually release, few of them seem to have a clear picture in their minds of what correct, balanced body action looks like—or feels like. In their misdirected efforts to get some power into the swing via the body, ninety-five out of a hundred players sway as they take the club back.   That is, they move the bulk of their weight to the right in such a way that they push themselves off balance immediately.   That sway finishes the chance there and then for a correct swing and a good shot.   The rest of the swing is a rushed attempt to compensate for that first big error.

The best image, I think, for conveying the nonsway pivot (which sets up the desired exchange of weight) is the one Percy Boomer introduced years ago.   His advice—and I endorse it heartily—is for the player to imagine that he is standing inside a barrel about as wide as his stance.   Then the player must feel as he swings that he is turning inside that barrel, turning freely but without touching the right side of the barrel going back or the left side following through—or, for that matter, any side of the barrel.   This is the introductory step in getting the right concept of rotation.

Top of backswing

Address

Following through

5

3 | TIP FROM THE TOP

from **AL COLLINS**
Bahamas Country Club, Nassau,
and Sleepy Hollow Country Club,
Scarborough-on-Hudson, N. Y.

The Longer-Shafted Driver

ON ALMOST every golf course there are at least three or four holes where it is a distinct advantage to get the ball out a good, long distance from the tee. I am now fifty-nine years old, and in recent years I have found that I can no longer get that old yardage with standard-length drivers. Like any player who once was a fairly long hitter, I hated to give up that distance and play an old man's game, so two years ago I began experimenting with longer-shafted drivers. Of course, the idea was not original. Through the years many fine amateurs and pros—Bobby Cruickshank and Chick Evans among them— have used such clubs successfully.

I have come to the following conclusions about longer-shafted drivers: (*1*) They do indeed facilitate greater distance, especially for men over fifty. (*2*) The swing is easier to control. (*3*) Your swing pattern need not be altered.

Skipping the involved language of physics, it all boils down to this: The two ways you can gain greater distance are (*a*) by increasing the speed of your club head by speeding up your swing, or (*b*) by increasing the arc of your swing. The former is risky. It multiples the chances for error. Go with the latter. Keep your normal speed and increase your arc with a longer-shafted club.

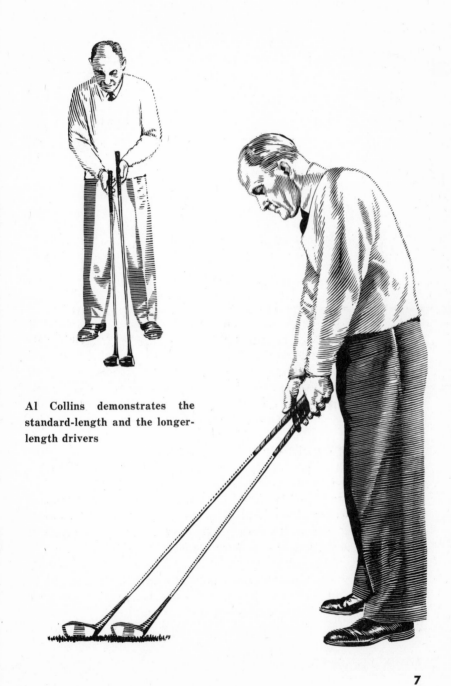

Al Collins demonstrates the standard-length and the longer-length drivers

7

4 | TIP FROM THE TOP

from SHELLEY MAYFIELD
Meadow Brook Club, Westbury, N. Y.

The Left Heel

AMONG our fine professionals, it has become standard practice—as uniform as the grip—to raise the left heel only a shade on the backswing. When they are playing the six-iron through the wedge, the left heel never leaves the ground. On a full shot with a driver, calling for the fullest pivot, the greatest exchange of weight, and the longest arc, the left heel is never lifted more than an inch and a half off the ground. There are, in fact, a few players, myself among them, who prefer to play all their shots without ever raising the left heel off the ground.

My reason for calling this to your attention is that most average golfers have the habit of lifting the left heel far too much on the backswing, sometimes as high as five inches. This tends to pull the golfer's head "off the ball" as he nears the top of the backswing. Furthermore, when you lift the left heel too high, nine out of ten times on the downswing you will return it to the right or left of the position it occupied when you started your swing. Replacing your heel an inch to the right or left can change your line of flight as much as twenty yards. On the other hand, raising the left heel the bare minimum is a major step towards achieving consistency and greater firmness at impact.

Incorrect: heel
lifted much too
high

Correct: heel lifted
only slightly

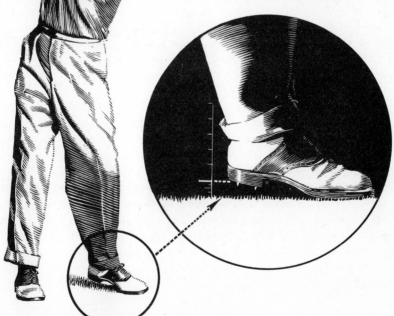

TIP
FROM
THE
TOP

from **HAROLD SARGENT**
East Lake Country Club,
Atlanta, Ga.

The Straight Left Arm

THE PART played by the left arm—the controlling factor in the good golf swing—starts at address. The left arm should be neither stiff, rigid, nor locked in joint at the elbow but should be comfortably extended. Throughout the backswing, it should remain firm and extended, for this enables a golfer to maintain the wide arc that builds up power and, moreover, promotes accuracy by helping to groove the same arc on swing after swing.

As many of us see it, the start of the downswing is probably the most crucial part of the entire swing. At this point many golfers make the costly error of letting the left arm virtually collapse. When this happens, the right hand, arm, and side immediately take charge. Once in their grip, the player has no other alternative than to hit "from the top of his swing." He moves the club outside the correct line, and consequently he has to pull it back across the line of flight as he contacts the ball. The result of this hitting from the top is a slice, if the club face is open, a pull or a pulled hook, if the club face is shut. How do you avoid this? Make certain your left arm remains the controlling factor as you start down from the top of the backswing.

Correct Incorrect   Correct Incorrect

The correct position at the
top of the backswing. Left
arm must stay in control as
golfer begins downswing

from **RAY GAFFORD**
Ridglea Country Club,
Fort Worth, Texas

The Chip and Run

I N THIS AGE of soft, heavily watered greens, the lofted approach with the nine-iron or wedge has become standard for most golfers. Many automatically play this type of shot even when the situation calls for the old run-up method, the chip and run. Many more golfers should know how to play the chip-and-run short approach than now do, for a golfer can really obtain more control by running the ball up toward the hole than by attempting to drop it in the hole.

The chip-and-run shot is played with any iron from the four through the nine, the club selected depending on the lie of the land. For all clubs the technique is exactly the same. The club face is square to the line at address, with the hands slightly ahead of the ball. The club strikes the ball a descending blow. There should be only a minimum of wrist action when the player takes the club back; and on the forward part of the stroke there should be no wrist action at all.

The idea, of course, is to pitch the ball a short distance in the air and to let it roll the rest of the way to the hole. The player learns how to gauge the length of the shot by practice and by carefully observing how the ball performs. A good shot is one that is played the right distance.

Ray Gafford advocates using very little wrist action on backswing
on chip and run, none whatsoever on the forward part of the stroke

7 | TIP FROM THE TOP

from **HARRY COOPER**
Metropolis Country Club,
White Plains, N. Y.

Checking the Head Position

THAT OLD admonition, "Keep your eye on the ball," is not nearly so meaningful as it has often been conceded to be. The key point is not merely to keep your eye on the ball but to keep your head firmly anchored throughout your swing. Why is this so important? Well, the head serves as the pivotal center of the swing. As long as the head remains still and steady —and assuming your swing is built on a fundamentally sound action—you cannot fail to hit fine golf shots. However, if you move your head, you throw the center of your pivotal action off center; and this forces you to set up a series of compensations in your swing. You can get away with a swing made up of compensations now and then, but you are really defeating yourself in the long run. Consistently good golf can be produced only by sound, correct action.

One excellent method for testing whether or not you are keeping your head steady is to line it up on some nearby object, like a tree. Then stop when you are about halfway into your backswing and check whether or not your head has maintained that alignment. When the sun is out, the check is made much simpler. Then you line up your "shadow head" on some object like a tee marker and check whether or not it strays off the mark as you move into your backswing motion.

Address

Correct

Faulty

15

from **JOHN THOREN**
Myopia Hunt Club,
So. Hamilton, Mass.

The Waiter's Position

THE BEST METHOD I have found for teaching a golfer to hit the ball "from the inside out" is to establish a mental picture of the top of the backswing as being just about the position in which a waiter carries a trayful of glasses. He carries the tray with his right palm up, and that is relatively the position for the right hand in the perfect golf swing.

The start of the swing is very important in getting you to the proper "waiter's position." The golfer who wants to overcome the common habit of hitting from the top or of hitting from the outside in and slicing the shot can establish the mental picture of the waiter very easily. He should start the swing with the right elbow tucked well into the side and should keep the elbow as close to that position as possible during the backswing.

The waiter's position sets up a slight reverse hand action as the club starts down. From this position the player can move into the shot and be sure of staying inside the ball (or of hitting from the inside out, as the expression goes). This also keeps a player from expending his power too soon and brings him into the hitting area in an excellent position to strike the ball accurately and forcefully.

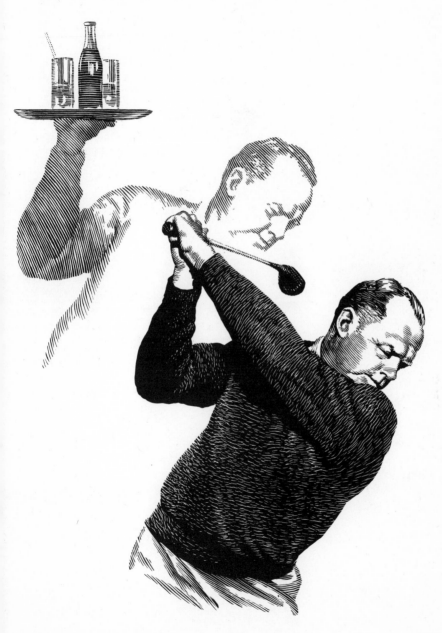

17

9

TIP
FROM
THE
TOP

from **PALMER MAPLES**
Benvenue Country Club,
Rocky Mount, N. C.

The Towel and the Right Elbow

IT'S BEEN my experience that it is not beneficial to point out all his faults to a golfer but to try to isolate a key error he is making. If we can correct that one, at the same time we usually correct a good many subsidiary faults that spring from that major error.

Very often, assuming that a golfer's grip and stance are correct, where a good many players seem to go wrong fundamentally is in turning the control of the swing over to the right hand and arm from the beginning of the stroke. I have long made it a point to suggest to my pupils that they spend some time on the practice fairway working on an old tip I still consider a first-class antidote for this particular error. What you do is take a towel, tie a knot in the middle of it, and stick the knot under your right armpit. To keep the towel from falling to the ground as you move into your backswing, you must keep that right elbow fairly snug against your right side. When you do this—and this is the point—your left arm and side have to take the club back. This is what they should do, of course.

This tip yields a golfer two other dividends: (*1*) It helps you to develop a wide arc to your swing. And (*2*) it also builds the kind of action in which your right arm and side are in an ideal position to swing through the ball as you enter the hitting area on the downswing.

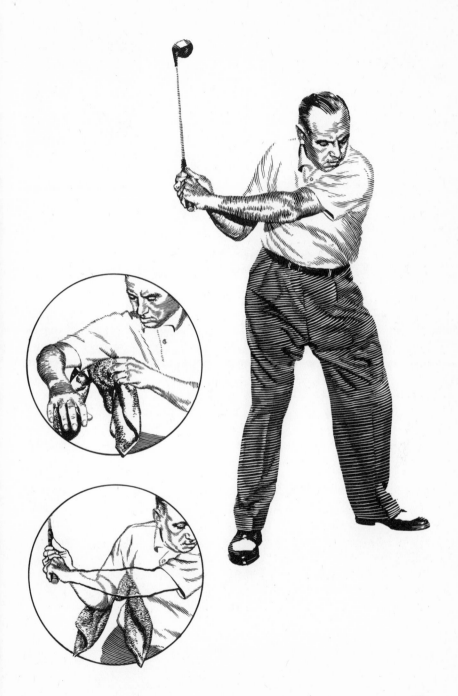

TIP
FROM
THE
TOP

from **BYRON NELSON**
Fairway Ranch, Roanoke, Texas

Going Back

THE AVERAGE GOLFER is subject to three fundamental faults when he takes the club back: (*1*) picking the club up too quickly with his hands, rather than swinging the club back along the line; (*2*) pulling the club up too close to the body; and (*3*) starting the body action before the hands and the golf club start to move—which pulls the body out of line and forces the golfer into an unbalanced chopping action.

When I first began playing, I brought the club back too close on the backswing, and this caused me to hook and shank. To overcome this fault, I drew a mental line straight back from the ball, and also in front of the ball, to reinforce my awareness of the line of flight—the line I intended the ball to travel. Then I worked on drawing the club back along that line.

Today my habit is to pick an object in the foreground that is situated on the line of flight—a tree or a bunker or a house. Then I take the club back straight from that object and the ball. To check my backswing in practice, I stick a tee about six or eight inches behind the ball on the intended line of flight. And when I draw the club back I can check to see whether the club hits the tee squarely or whether it tips or shanks it.

Incorrect: club pulled
up too close to the body

Correct: club is taken back on straight
line from the ball, with the hands, the
club, and the body moving cohesively

*from***AL COLLINS**
Bahamas Country Club, Nassau,
and Sleepy Hollow Country Club,
Scarborough-on-Hudson, N. Y.

The Approach Putt

T HERE IS really no need for those 8's and 9's incurred by golfers who regularly play around 100 and sometimes play in the low 90's. They are caused by plain poor sense: the golfer tries to overpower the ball off the tee; he plays the ball improperly from a hazard, refusing to accept the penalty because ten years ago he hit a phenomenal recovery from a trap with a spoon; he tries to hole every putt in sight and, as often as not, takes three putts.

Let us concern ourselves here with only this last unnecessary error. When the average golfer is fifteen feet or more from the cup, his ambition should be to get down comfortably in two putts. He can do this very easily, even when he is forty feet or so away, if he gives his primary attention to stroking the putt the right distance. A helpful tip in this connection is to visualize the cup as the center of a circle some five feet in diameter and to concentrate on rolling the approach putt so that it comes to rest within this imaginary circle. This leaves you only a two-and-a-half-footer to hole to get down to two. My old friend Mrs. Opal Hill was a wonderful putter because she never charged the hole and always kept her sense of distance at the front of her mind on making her approach putts. The result was that she wouldn't 3-putt three greens in a year.

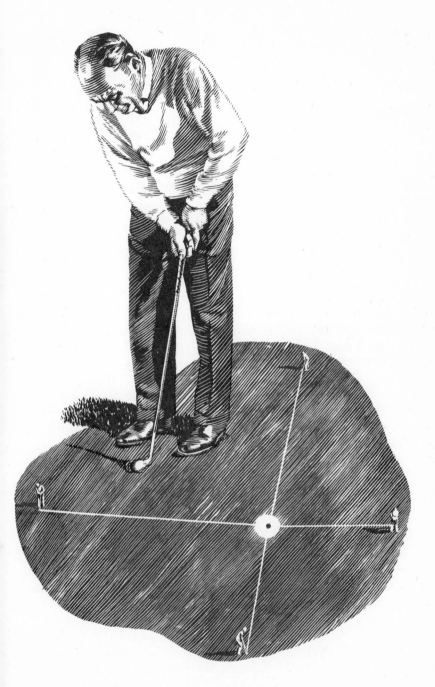

12	TIP FROM THE TOP

from **DENNY LAVENDER**
Cedar Crest Golf Club, Dallas, Texas

The Hands and the Line of the Shoulders

IDEALLY, the head of the club in a good swing describes a nearly perfect circle around the body of the golfer, with the shoulders as the fulcrum.   To come close to swinging in this circular path is hard work—the bane of the average golfer's existence. His difficulty starts at the very beginning of the swing when he brings the club back from address.   If the golfer will concentrate on executing one simple fundamental, he can assure himself of a good circular swing.   It is this: At the top of the backswing, the hands must be brought back behind the line of the shoulders and the head.

If the hands are brought that far behind the player, the left arm will be straightened, the shoulders will rotate as the hips turn—more or less automatically—and the golfer's weight will shift naturally back to his right foot at the top of the backswing.   All a golfer has to concentrate on is getting his hands behind him, and the other correct moves are set up.

Most faulty swings result from the player's taking his hands up without bringing them sufficiently behind his shoulders and his head—or, to say it another way, from keeping his hands too far out in front at the top of his backswing.

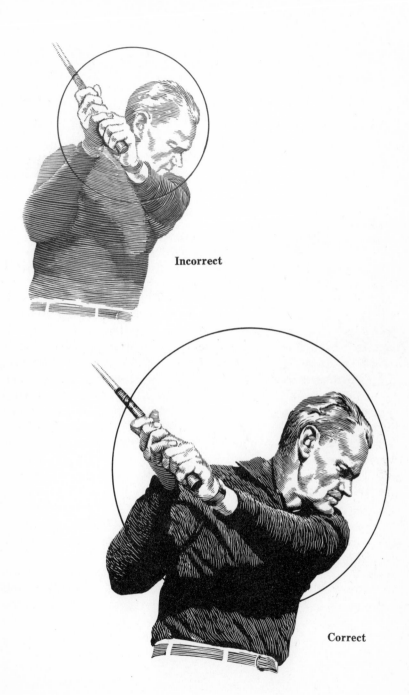

Incorrect

Correct

25

TIP

FROM

THE

TOP

from **JIMMY D'ANGELO**
Dunes Golf and Beach Club,
Myrtle Beach, S. C.

Lobbing the Pitch

A SHORT approach to a fast green guarded by traps presents an interesting challenge with rewarding satisfactions. To hold the green by means of backspin (developed by punching the ball into the turf) requires considerable practice and skill, possibly more than the average golfer can bring to his occasional rounds. Accordingly, it's a wise decision for golfers to cultivate the lob type of approach, a shot which reduces the percentage of error and which does the job very well, too. When correctly executed, the lobbed pitch sends the ball up to the green in a very steep trajectory. The ball drops almost vertically onto the green, and little roll results.

In playing this shot, use a nine-iron or a pitching wedge. Take your stance with the ball an inch or so farther forward than usual. Allow yourself a backswing somewhat longer than you would use if you were planning to spank a backspin approach the same distance and allow your wrists to cock freely. Swing smoothly and well through the ball. You will find that the ball will get up very quickly and sit down very well when it plops onto the green.

This shot can be easily learned with a little practice and can be just as effective as the much more exacting backspin shot.

The ball is played slightly
farther forward than usual

In following through, do not
whip the club around but let
it go out toward the hole

Allow yourself a liberal
backswing

14 | TIP FROM THE TOP

from **HARRY COOPER**
Metropolis Country Club,
White Plains, N. Y.

Spotting the Ball

THERE'S BEEN a decided trend of late towards playing all shots (from the wedge right down to the wooden clubs) with the ball spotted in just about the same position with reference to its distance between the left and right heels. For pro stars who can practice eight hours a day, this ultra-uniformism works out all right. They are able to acquire great feel and to compensate with their hand action for the slight differences between the contact point of one club and another. But this method is very harmful for the average golfer. If you don't move the ball, you must indeed change your hand action a bit for every different club, and this is well beyond the average golfer's ability. Uniform spotting gets him into all sorts of trouble.

It is much more sensible to graduate the position of the ball to fit the varying physical properties of each club—playing the key club, the five-iron, in the center of the stance and moving the ball back about an eighth of a turn as the loft of the club increases, an eighth of a turn forward as the loft decreases. In this way you accomplish your adjustment immediately, and there is no need to compensate with your hand action when you execute your swing.

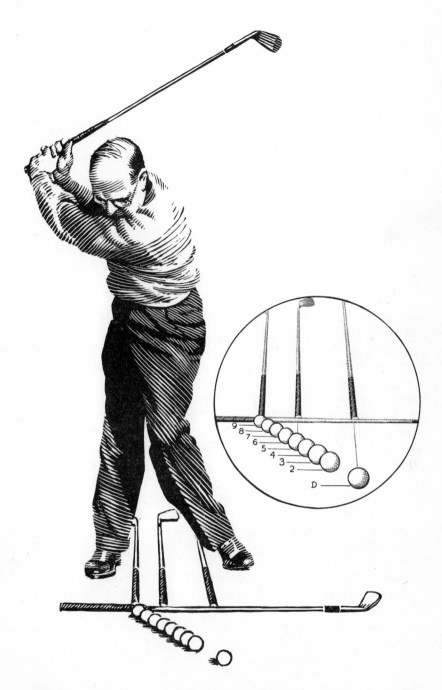

15 | TIP FROM THE TOP

from **ED DUDLEY**
Augusta National Golf Club,
Augusta, Ga.

The Grip and the Swing

A S PARADOXICAL as it may sound, relaxed, well-played golf is
a "pressure game"! Pressure, as properly applied by the
fingers as they grip the club shaft, is in my opinion one of the
fundamental factors underlying good golf. In fact, the position of the hands on the club is the principal key to control,
and only through control can a golfer rise above the dub stage.

How much pressure? How applied? Well, the pressure
should be that amount that provides a "feel" of the club without producing tenseness. It should be applied by the last three
fingers of the left hand. Or, to put it another way, the hands
are not supposed to be limp on the club but in a position where
they feel ready to do their work: to act as the swivel of the
swing, to control the takeaway as the club starts on its backswing, to start the downmove on the downswing.

The proper grip—meaning that the pressure of the fingers is
right as well as the position they occupy on the shaft—permits
the all-important cocking of the wrists at the top of the swing,
eliminating tenseness in the wrists and forearms. It also tends
to produce a straight but not unnaturally stiff left arm. It is
worth your while to get this grip fundamental right, for it is
the foundation on which all the other actions are built.

30

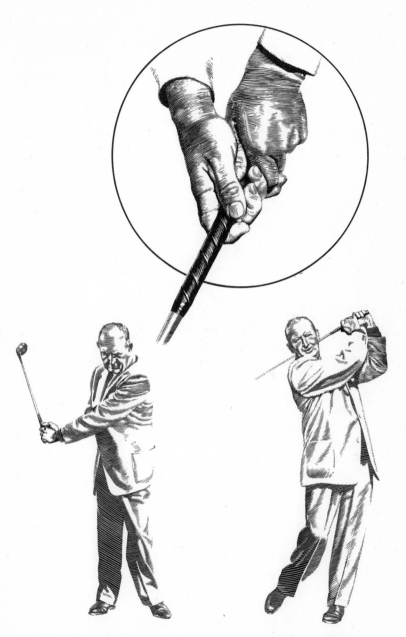

The correct movements on the backswing and the downswing
can be executed only if the hands are properly on the club

31

TIP
FROM
THE
TOP

from **SHELLEY MAYFIELD**
Meadow Brook Club, Westbury, N. Y.

The Right Shoulder and Elbow

MANY AVERAGE GOLFERS I have watched defeat their purpose at the very beginning of the stroke: they address the ball with their shoulders level, the right raised as high as the left. If you think things over for a moment, you will realize that the left hand grips the club a full hand's length higher along the shaft than the right hand does. With both shoulders level and both arms extended, it follows that, if your left arm is extended comfortably, the right will be strained and rigid. This is exactly opposite to what you want in golf: you want a straight left arm and a relaxed right arm.

At address a golfer's right shoulder should hang three or four inches lower than his left. This enables the right arm to be in a relatively relaxed position. In turn, the right elbow, when it is not overextended stiffly at address, will be in a position where it can perform its correct function. On the backswing, the right elbow "folds" close to the body so that, at the top of the backswing, the straight line between the right wrist and elbow points vertically toward the ground and not horizontally toward the horizon. It is really quite impossible for a golfer to move into the proper hitting position if his right elbow is "floating" incorrectly at the top of the backswing.

The position of address is an active part of the swing. The arms, hands, and shoulders naturally seek to return to the approximate position of address when they enter the hitting area.

32

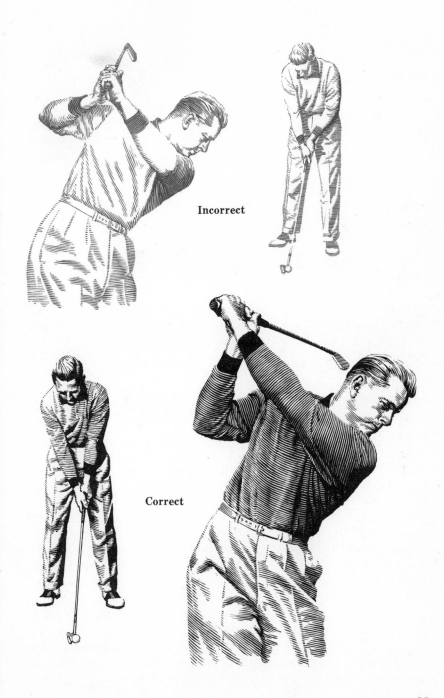

Incorrect

Correct

33

from **BABE ZAHARIAS**

Guarding Against Slugging

During my career in golf I have seen countless poor shots caused by all kinds of errors. However, if I were asked to name the one chief error that undermines both the high- and low-handicap players, I would without hesitation nominate the almost universal striving for greater distance. Though I am a naturally long hitter, I have been subject myself to this fault from time to time, so I know from my own experience how disastrous it can be. By pressing for extra distance you hope to gain added yardage, but what happens is that you lose your balance and your timing, and all you gain are added woes: O.B. & P.L.—Out of Bounds and Probably Lost.

When I was a young girl just setting out in golf, I knew that my appeal for the spectators was my ability to smack the ball farther than a good many low-handicap men players. All I did for a while was to try to hit the ball a mile. I made my point. I was known as a long hitter. But I was so erratic that I wasn't really much of a golfer. It was only when I got some common sense and started to build a sound swing on a sound foundation that I began to become a player.

TIP FROM THE TOP

from **AL ESPOSITO**
Country Club of Charleston, S. C.

Bankside Lies

ONE SHOT many golfers have a misconception about is the recovery from an uphill bank in the rough that fringes the green area. It is really quite a simple shot. In taking your stance—which is the key to making the shot simple—the golfer should bend his left knee to compensate for the incline of the slope and should play the ball just slightly forward of the center of his body. The right shoulder should be down a bit, but the incline usually takes care of that anyhow.

The golfer should step up to this shot understanding that it is a member of the chip-shot family. The common error golfers make is to pick the club up steeply on the backswing and to force the hands quickly up and over on the follow-through, as though all the stroke required were a punch-scoop delivered with all possible strength. What this faulty technique accomplishes is to drive the ball into the bank. Instead, the golfer should understand that he is playing the stroke correctly when there is only slight wrist-break action and when the back of his left hand goes straight out toward the pin, as it does on an ordinary chip. The club head should stay low, merely following the up-slope of the bank. The angle of the club face provides all the loft that is needed. It is up to the golfer to provide the delicacy the shot calls for.

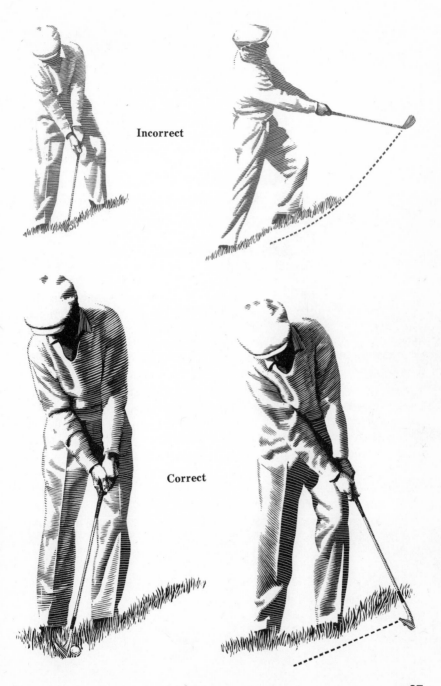

Incorrect

Correct

37

from **MIKE SOUCHAK**
Grossinger, N. Y.

The Crucial Four-Footer

LIKE ALL professional golfers, I have tried to work out a set of fundamental procedures for keeping my putting strokes as consistent and as reliable as I can make them. Staying with these fundamentals has helped me a good deal, particularly in holing the short ones—those crucial four-footers that make or break a golf round more than any other shot in the game.

As for the grip, I've discovered that I have a much better touch if my right hand rides high on the shaft. Besides eliminating the tendency to pull the putt, this position helps me to get a uniform speed on the ball.

As far as address goes, I find it valuable to use a slight forward press of the hands before taking the blade back. Too much of a forward press can be bad, because a golfer then tends to jab the ball down into the grass. A slight forward press makes it easier for the left hand to go through the ball after contact, to move a little more out toward the hole. This, I find, enables you to get the slow speed on the ball that's so desirable. As for my right hand, I like to feel that the right palm is moving straight along the line of the putt to the hole.

The slight forward
press at address

The left hand contin-
ues through the ball

TIP
FROM
THE
TOP

from **PATTY BERG**
St. Andrews, Ill.

Getting the Right Hip out of the Way

SINCE WOMEN don't have as powerful hands as men do, they can't get away with a poorly executed swing nearly so well. In order to develop adequate hitting power, a woman must master really good footwork and body action; and she must tie these together with rhythm and timing. The catch here is that comparatively few women seem to understand the difference between correct body action—based on pivoting— and incorrect body action—where the sway is ruinous.

Since the word pivot seems to confuse most women golfers rather than present them with a clear picture of what they should do, perhaps a better way to get the point across is to put it this way: on the backswing, you do not slide your body laterally from left to right, *you coil your body away from the ball.* The key to coiling correctly, the way I think of it, is to get the right hip out of the way. This movement, the rotation of the right hip to the rear, is actually started by the left side. If there ever was a shortcut to proper body action, this is it: getting the right hip out of the way. If you do that, you won't sway and you won't be stuck off balance at the top of a faulty backswing with nothing but a feeble pair of hands to chop at the ball.

One thing more. Keep your head still. If you move your head off the ball, you'll probably move your body along with it.

Incorrect:
the lateral sway

Correct:
the right hip rotates

The strong coiled position at the top of the backswing

from **JOHNNY PALMER**
Tulsa Country Club, Tulsa, Okla.

The Simplified Putting Stroke

WHEN PUTTING TECHNIQUES are dissected and discussed, it strikes me that perhaps too little is said about the role timing plays. Granted that the putting stroke calls for a different execution from the tee-to-green strokes, nevertheless it requires the same sense of timing that the longer shots do.

In this day and age when people are happiest if you can reveal to them some "inside" shortcut to success, I realize how commonplace it must seem to golfers to remind them that they must work on their timing above all. Nevertheless, it is what puts the ball into the hole, and the various mannerisms the top putters employ simply help the individual to refine his timing. For myself, putting is, and has always been, the application of a few tried-and-true, old-fashioned precepts. The weight is a shade forward. With my line decided on, I work on getting the right speed. I try to take the putter back with both hands, directly on the line. I try to hit the ball solidly, square. I let the club head go right toward the hole.

When I fall into a spell of below-standard putting, it is generally because I am picking the putter up on the backswing and throwing my timing and my stroke off. When I check my grip at these times, I am almost certain to find that I have let my left hand slide off to the left. Turning the left hand more on top, where it should be, helps me to get back on the right path.

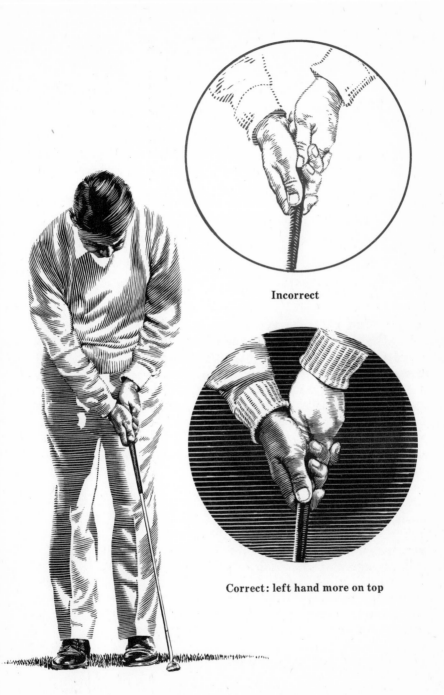

Incorrect

Correct: left hand more on top

from **EDDIE WILLIAMS**
Louisville Country Club,
Louisville, Ky.

Developing Live Hands

YOU WILL never see a good golfer with "dead" hands. The connection between the golfer and the club must be a live, flexible union. If not, everything good about his footwork and body action will be nullified.

Some golfers grasp the club so tightly that their hand action is deadened. Others grasp it so loosely that there can be no hand action at all. Under such obstructing circumstances, all a golfer can do is to hack stiff-armed at the ball, or at the other extreme, be so loose that the natural wrist and hand action that would result from a good, firm, live grip are not set up to function.

Live hands mean strong hands. Strong hands can be developed through proper exercises with the golf club, indoors and out. The illustrations on page 45 show the proper grip and the proper movements for strengthening weak arms and forearms. The stronger the hands, the easier it is to execute good golf shots without tension or strain. When the average golfer learns how to use his hands properly from the time he picks up the club until the finish of his swing, then and only then will he be able to work into a uniform, rhythmic swing.

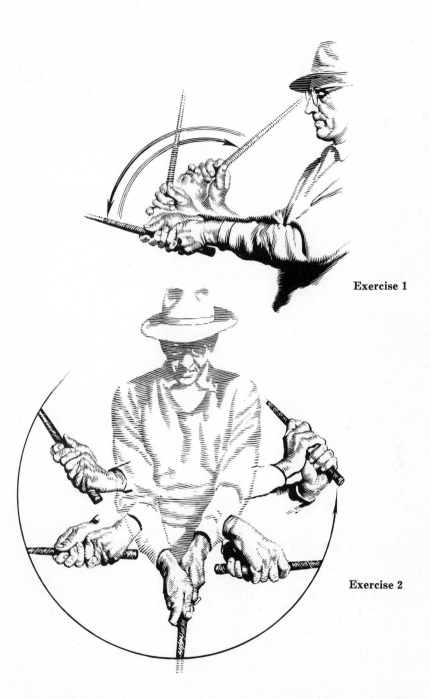

Exercise 1

Exercise 2

23 | TIP FROM THE TOP

from **GEORGE CORCORAN**
Greensboro Country Club,
Greensboro, N. C.

The Wider Stance for Women

THE AVERAGE woman golfer addresses the ball on the tee a little self-consciously; swings as though she is afraid that either her arms, the club, or the ball might break; and sends a looping little blooper of a drive slicing toward the rough on the right of the fairway. Why?

The reason is that she won't swing hard enough at the ball. Even if she wanted to, she couldn't, because she isn't set for it. Whether from inherent modesty or conscious worry about her skirt, the average woman golfer doesn't take a wide enough stance to be able to cut loose with a good swing at the ball.

At address the feet should be so planted that the outside of the heels are the width of the shoulders apart. This wider, firmer stance gives the golfer better balance and will enable her to move her hips normally as she pivots. By standing correctly the woman golfer can swing harder—more through the ball. This will give her five or ten yards more distance because it increases the speed of the club head at impact. Swinging harder will also give women golfers straighter shots. Ninety per cent of women golfers slice because of their defensive attitude. Swinging away, more through the ball, gives the club head the chance it needs to meet the ball squarely at the bottom of the swing.

46

Incorrect:
stance too narrow

Correct stance

| ## TIP
FROM
THE
TOP

from **CHARLES McKENNA**
Oak Hill Country Club,
Pittsford, N. Y.

The Fundamental Chip Shot

IT'S A RARE DAY when you'll see an average golfer practicing approach shots, chip shots, or trap shots. And that is one of the many reasons why his game doesn't improve. If he does deign to practice, the driver is his weapon. He won't relinquish the idea that a 250-yard drive is the game's biggest thrill. This is not the attitude of the good golfer. He would rather run up a fine chip shot for his birdie or par any time.

When you are chipping from thirty yards out, you can use a six-, seven-, eight-, or nine-iron. The particular club depends for the most part on your preference, with due respect, of course, to the lie of the ball and the terrain you are dealing with. But the stance and the club action are fundamentally the same in all cases. Use an open stance—the left foot back slightly from the line of the shot. Keep the weight more on the left foot than on the right. Bend the knees a bit so that you feel an inclination to sit. Don't pick the club up on the backswing. Brush it away from the ball, keeping the wrists firm so that the stroke doesn't become wobbly. Try not to hurry or to poke the ball, and don't try to lift the ball. The club will do that for you. And after you have contacted the ball, let the club head swing out toward the hole.

Above: the golfer's wrists are kept firm
on the backswing.   At right: the length
of the follow-through should be about
equal to the length of the backswing

from **JACK BURKE, JR.**
Kiamesha Lake, N. Y.

Hit That Cloud!

MY EXPERIENCE, as a now fairly veteran tournament player, has brought home to me that, regardless of some minor things I may or may not be doing on a given round, my game will be fundamentally sound if I stay under the shot.

To explain this a bit: there is always a tendency when you are aiming for a pin situated on the same level with yourself, to try and line the ball on a low, bullet-like flight for the target. When you have this conception in your mind of the shot you're going to play, you're likely to overaccelerate the whole action at contact and to hammer the ball so that it slides to the right, ducks a little to the left—or, at any rate, does something erratic.

When I find I'm doing this—and, I hope, sometimes before an error informs me—I try to remind myself that a shot that flies in a high trajectory seldom goes crooked. Instead of setting my eyes on the pin, I raise them and pick out some higher object behind the pin as my target—the top of a tree, a spot on a slope, or even a cloud. Then, by swinging in such a way that my shot will soar toward that object, I will move into the ball with an action that encourages staying under the shot. I am convinced that there's tremendous value in keeping this image, this precept, always in the forefront of my mind.

from **LOUISE SUGGS**
Sea Island, Ga.

Lining Up the Shot

O NE FUNDAMENTAL FAULT that I have observed to be shared by many women golfers is that they start with their hands behind the ball at address and, consequently, have their hands in a weak position throughout their swing.

The error begins when a player lines up faultily. In the process of lining up her hands with the club face and also with the target, a golfer tends to get her hands behind the club face in the act of placing the club behind the ball to sight the line. After obtaining her line, she forgets to get her hands back in front of the club face. Having the hands in front is more important than is generally understood. It sets up a strong left side, with the left hand the leader at all times. It leads to a more natural cock of the wrists on the backswing and a more natural body turn. With the hands behind, the right hand is in a position to take charge, thus introducing many errors. The golfer will pull the club too far inside or pick it up too sharply, and will generally fall into a strained incorrect position at the top and into a lurching approach to impact.

When you are getting the hands set at address, that is the time to extend the left arm comfortably. You won't overswing, but you will be in a fully extended position at the top.

Incorrect: hands behind

Correct: hands ahead

53

from **SAM SNEAD**
Greenbrier Golf and Country Club,
White Sulphur Springs, W. Va.

The Importance of Relaxed Legs

BEING TENSE ruins more golf shots for more players than any other thing. When a golfer is all tightened up, he doesn't have a chance to swing correctly at the ball. These unrelaxed golfers figure that the faster they swing the more distance they'll get, and you've seen hundreds of them who go back as fast as they come down. They're the boys who have inspired that popular hustler's slogan: "Give me a man with a fast backswing and a fat wallet."

Rhythm and timing are the most important things in a golf swing. You can't get them—you can't even come close to getting them—unless you're relaxed; and I mean relaxed not only in the arms and hands but throughout the body, especially through the legs. Walter Hagen used to say that as long as he could keep his legs relaxed he didn't worry. The rest would take care of itself. I agree with him one hundred per cent. When your legs and ankles are nice and supple, only then will your muscles be able to do the work you want them to do. Only then can you pivot right and get that sense of rhythm that helps you to go back in one piece and to start down from the top with everything moving in close harmony.

The golfer with tensed
legs cannot pivot

The tied-up golfer is
necessarily off balance
through the ball

Relaxation leads to the desired actions

from **GRAHAM ROSS**
Dallas Athletic Club Country Club,
Dallas, Texas

The Left-Hand Grip

THE BALANCE AND FEEL of a golf club are transmitted to the player through the hands. Few golfers understand as clearly as they should which parts of the palm and fingers do the actual gripping. To put it another way, they remain hazy about which muscles of the hand hold the club, exert the pressure, and, by their position and action, initiate the golf swing and influence its execution.

In regard to the left hand's grip on the shaft, I should like to propose that a golfer think for a minute about the way he picks up a pitcher of water. The last three fingers of your hand grip the handle of the pitcher. They're the ones that lift it and hold it. The thumb and index finger, however, are relaxed—you could hold a pencil or a golf ball between them and your grip on the pitcher wouldn't be affected.

That is how you should grip the golf club with the left hand. The last three fingers provide the power to lift and swing the club; they remain glued to the shaft. The thumb and index finger are applied to the shaft much more lightly. They provide as little or as much pressure as is necessary on those shots in which touch is important.

56

Graham Ross illustrates the correct left-hand grip

from **BETTY JAMESON**
San Antonio Country Club,
San Antonio, Texas

Securing the Stance in Traps

GOLFERS who customarily take pains to obtain a firm, correct stance before hitting their shots go to sleep frequently in this department when confronted with recovering from a bunker. I have in mind those times when the ball lies within the concave dip of a bunker in such a position that the player must stand a few inches above it or below it.

Although there isn't much that a player can do about his stance if the ball lies *above* him—aside from making sure that he is properly balanced—he can greatly enhance his chances of a good shot when the ball lies *below* him if he will shovel his feet into the sand until they are down to the same level as the ball. He can then move into hitting the shot without "dropping" his swing inches below its normal plane in order to make the desired contact with the ball or the sand behind the ball.

The next time you are faced with this predicament, simply take your regular stance. Then, as you line yourself up and soak in the shot generally, squidge your heels back and forth in the sand until your feet and the ball are resting on the same level. You will probably play better trap shots; and really you should, since you've made the shot an appreciably easier one.

Preparatory stance   Feet shoveled in

TIP
FROM
THE
TOP

from **BILL SHIELDS**
Thorny Lea Golf Club,
Brockton, Mass.

Hitting Through Instead of Down

B OBBY JONES played our course thirty-two years ago, played it for ten days. I've watched all the great golfers from Alec Smith to Dr. Middlecoff, but I learned more from watching Jones than any other golfer. I'll tell you what impressed me the most: he shifted his weight beautifully. He never hit down; he hit through the ball.

I've been trying to get this across to my pupils for years, but it's tough. They hear that the pros hit down on the ball, so that's what they're going to do too. Only they do it wrong. They don't hit the ball on the downswing, in the process of swinging through, like the pros. They hammer down on the ball as if they were banging a nail into wood. They get into the bad habit of playing the ball too close to the right foot; and from that position they can't develop good hand action.

A very fine golfer will get more distance on his irons by playing the ball a little back, but the average golfer will dig. If he would play the ball in line with his left heel on all his shots, he'd hit through then. One more thing. You won't see real good golfers like the doctor taking a big hunk of turf to control their swing. They don't have to. They've already got their swing under control.

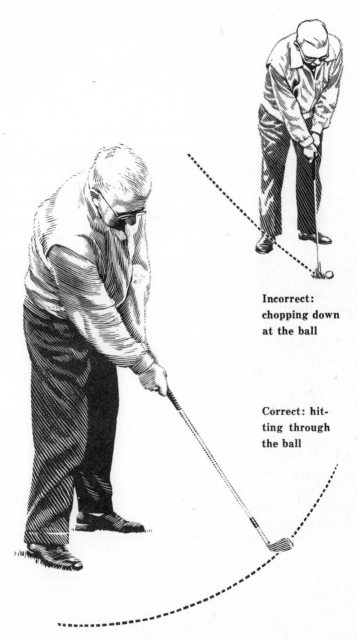

Incorrect:
chopping down
at the ball

Correct: hit-
ting through
the ball

61

31 | TIP FROM THE TOP

from **ED OLIVER**
Blue Hill Country Club,
Canton, Mass.

Avoiding Flatness

THE MAJOR PROBLEM for chunky men in golf is keeping their swing from being too flat—that is, on too shallow or horizontal a plane. The first thing they must learn in order to avoid this flatness is to take a more restricted pivot. Employing a slightly open stance helps considerably to cut down an excessive body turn. So does concentrating on taking the club back on a straight line from the ball, since it leads the player into a more upright swing. As the illustration shows, I recommend that when heavily built golfers practice, they place a club parallel to the line of flight as a visual aid to coming back straight on the line.

I am strictly a hands-player myself. But even for the average golfer of chunky physique I advocate the short, upright swing with the emphasis on firmness and timing. Don't let your left arm get stiff at address. Make sure your shoulders come underneath your chin, not out and around your chin. As for stances, I have found I get the best results by playing the woods with an open stance, the medium irons from a square stance, and the short irons from a slightly open stance.

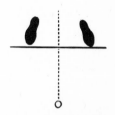

Stance for medium irons

For short irons

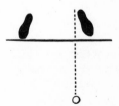

For woods

63

32 | TIP FROM THE TOP

from **PHIL PERKINS**
Highland Park Golf Club,
Cleveland, Ohio

Trap-Shot Hand Action

I WOULD LIKE to recommend a safe and simple technique for exploding out of traps. It is primarily a right-hand shot, and these are the key points to observe: The ball is played off the left heel. The blade is open. The left hand is turned well to the left on the shaft, with no knuckles showing. The backswing is upright, with a quick and full cock of the wrists. The downswing speed of the club head governs the distance you want the ball to carry. The bottom edge of the blade is aimed at a spot one inch behind the ball. You must be sure to stay down throughout the shot and to hit against a straight, non-turning left arm and hand as you cut through the sand under the ball.

Now here is the particular refinement I want to bring out. As it reaches the point just over the ball, the left hand slackens its forward motion—sort of "brakes" itself—but the right hand pushes through at normal speed. The "braking" of the left hand, and the push through of the right, cause the left hand to be forced open. Don't let this worry you. It is exactly the action you want. In other words, the heel of the left hand releases its grip on the club so that only the fingers of the left hand (and the full right hand) have hold of the club. The nice flicking motion this produces brings the ball out in a floating flight that has very little roll.

64

"Braking" the left arm forces heel of the
left hand off the shaft

**TIP
FROM
THE
TOP**

from **BUD HOLSCHER**
Apple Valley, Calif.

The Body Turn

A TALL PERSON naturally has a more upright swing than a more compactly built player like a Souchak or a Littler who can wheel his body around and swing comparatively "flat" with little or no effort. In trying for a less upright arc, the error tall players frequently fall into is to sway laterally—and then to overswing. What they should do is let their swing remain upright but work on developing a freer, better body turn.

The taller a man is, the more he thinks that his long arms and his hands can do the trick for him all by themselves. Consequently, the more inclined he is to get lazy about his legs and his body. He has it precisely wrong. He should give at least primary attention to the action of his legs and his body. When he is off his game, instead of searching for the fault somewhere in his arm and his hands, he should start with his feet and check the action of his swing literally from the ground up. If a golfer's feet are working properly, the chances are that his knees are working properly too, and so on up.

Horton Smith and Dutch Harrison are two tall men who come to mind who have tremendous body action. It goes a long way to explaining their considerable success, for correct body action is the great breeder of consistency.

Incorrect turn

Two views of the correct body turn

from **BETSY RAWLS**
Country Club of Spartansburg, S. C.

The Shoulder Turn

AN EXCEEDINGLY HIGH percentage of the women who play golf are slicers. They slice chiefly because they bring the club back with an improper shoulder turn. As they near the top of the backswing, instead of continuing to swing the club back and to turn the shoulders easily, they have a tendency to push their shoulders and arms up. Then, before they have completed the backswing, they start the downswing. Not only is their timing thrown off, but starting the club down from a position at the top where it points to the left side of the fairway is the invariable prelude to coming into the ball from the outside and cutting across it—slicing.

At the top of the backswing, the club, ideally, should be directly parallel to your intended line of flight, pointing, as it were, right at the target. If you have made a sufficient turn, your shoulders will be square. One excess, of course, is as bad as the other, and I would caution you about overturning the shoulders. This places the club in a position at the top where it is pointing to the right side of the fairway. A hooked shot generally results, for, if you overturn going back, you have to overturn to get back to the ball.

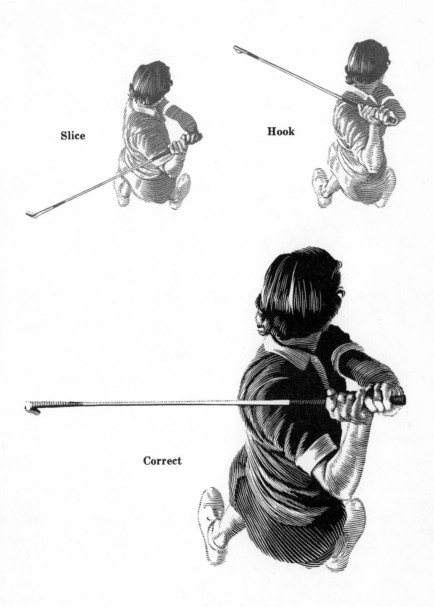

Slice

Hook

Correct

69

35

TIP FROM THE TOP

from **JOE LA MACHIA**
Locust Hill Country Club,
Pittsford, N. Y.

The Right-Hand Grip

T HE MOST COMMON FAULT I've noticed among high-handicap golfers is the placement of the right hand on the shaft. We all know that for right-handed players the right hand is much stronger than the left. Consequently, if the right hand is not positioned correctly, it will overpower the left. Too many golfers ruin their chances of playing the game well right off the reel when they "palm" the club in the right hand, tipping that hand well under the shaft. This makes the strong hand even stronger, wipes out the left almost completely, and produces a tremendous number of errors of all kinds.

When you take your overlapping grip, affix the right hand on the club so that the shaft does not lodge in the palm but is gripped by the fingers. (If you opened your hand, you would see the club lying diagonally across the fingers.) As for the right thumb, fold it over to the left side of the shaft so that it touches the middle finger and the forefinger—lightly. Almost immediately you will sense that the right hand feels different, that it feels weaker, and that the left feels stronger.

This stronger left hand will help you avoid picking the club up quickly on the backswing with a dominant right hand. The stronger left will not only stop your tendency to be an all-right-handed golfer but will also allow you to develop a more correct overall swing pattern. And then you have a chance to improve.

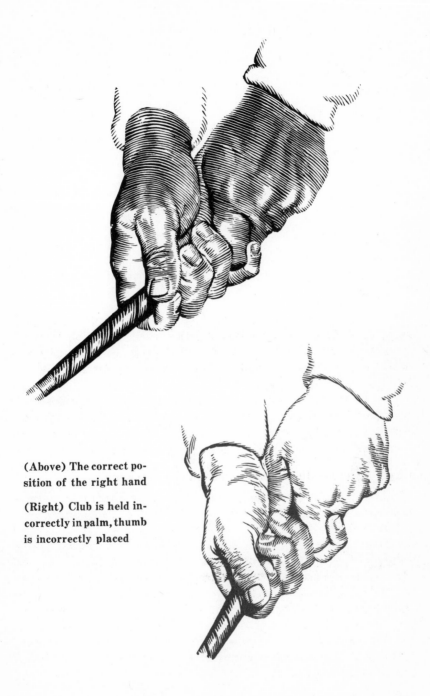

(Above) The correct position of the right hand

(Right) Club is held incorrectly in palm, thumb is incorrectly placed

71

36

TIP

FROM

THE

TOP

from **ARNOLD BROWNING**
Guyan Golf and Country Club,
Huntington, W. Va.

Reading the Grain of the Green

SINCE THIRTY TO FORTY-FIVE PER CENT of your total strokes are putts, whatever would improve your putting is worth your thought and study. An important part of putting understood by few average golfers is how to read the grain or the directional "nap" of a green.

Generally, the grass on any one green will be consistent in the direction of its growth. On some mountain and seaside courses the grasses on all the greens grow in the same direction. However, on most courses you will find an occasional green that is inconsistent in itself—the grass in one part of the green has an entirely different directional nap than the grass in another part of that same green. The most important place to look is around the cup, since the ball will be traveling slower there and will be more affected by the grain.

You can usually get a quick idea of the grain you're dealing with by looking at an area some ten to twenty feet from you. If it has a dark cast to it, you can figure that the grass is growing towards you. (Putting *against* the grain, you must tap the ball harder.) If the grass has a light, glossy sheen to it, you can figure that the grass is growing away from you. (Putting *with* the grain, you would naturally tap the ball a shade softer.) I think it is too complicating for the average golfer to bother unduly with crossgrains.

Against the grain

With the grain

from **ART WALL, JR.**
Pocono Manor, Penna.

Following Through in Putting

PUTTING is the most imprecise science in all of golf; and there are almost as many putting techniques as there are golfers. A technique I have found successful is to try to think of throwing my right palm out and into the hole. This helps me keep the putter blade square to the hole and prevents pulling or pushing the putt off line.

Successful putting is largely in the mind, anyway, and I find it helps give me the right mental image, the right feel, if I rest the putter shaft against the fleshy heel of my right palm. My left hand leads just slightly in the stroke, but when I have made a good putt, I feel the sense of the hit in that right palm.

I stand with my right elbow just barely touching my right hip—not resting on it, just brushing it. Then, if I concentrate on aiming my right palm for the hole, I usually find that I stroke the kind of putt I want. It seems to me that concentration, which is the absolute core of good putting, is made easier if the golfer focuses his attention on one detail only, whether it is this one or one of his own choosing.

Shaft rests against
heel of the right hand

Art Wall throws his
right palm "into" the
hole

75

TIP
FROM
THE
TOP

from **HELEN DETTWEILER**
Thunderbird Country Club,
Palm Springs, Calif.

The Wrist Turn

M OST WOMEN GOLFERS are extremely conscious of the importance of body action in the golf shot. But, probably because they have not had baseball training as many men have, they tend to ignore the importance of hand action. Actually, since the hands are the only part of the body to touch the club, they are super-important both in starting the swing and in controlling it throughout.

Your hands should set the club head in motion with a very gradual wrist cock and at the same time a slight *turn* of the left wrist. Remember this is a *turn*—not a roll or a pronation. Women, as well as men, tend to take the club back in an awkward stiff-wristed way which not only "hoods" the club (shuts the face) but also disastrously restricts the pivot.

The path of the club head should *not* be in a straight line away from the ball, but, because of the slight turn of the left wrist, should "angle back," following the arc the left hand naturally moves in as the body makes its accompanying turn. This correct wrist action will be especially helpful also in providing an inside-out path to your downswing—and that is the absolute essential of the straight golf shot.

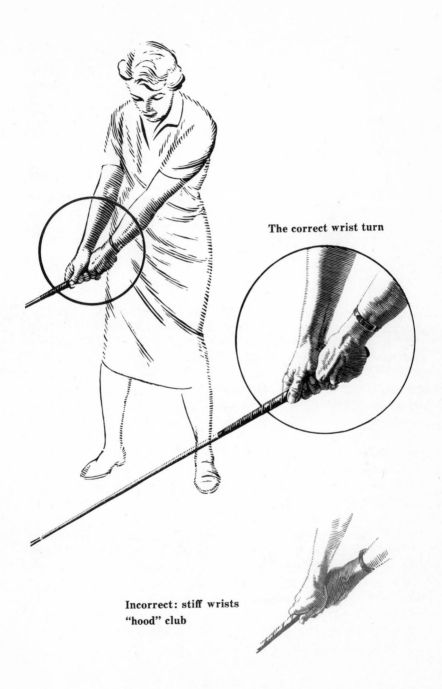

The correct wrist turn

Incorrect: stiff wrists
"hood" club

from **BYRON NELSON**
Roanoke, Texas

The Long Irons

BECAUSE the face of a long iron—the number one, two, or three—has so very little loft, it leads players to fear that they will not get the ball up into the air. The usual result is that the player tends to lift up with his body in the act of hitting the ball, instead of making sure that he stays down with the ball. And far from helping you to get the ball nicely into the air, this lifting up of the body produces a low-flying shot and very often a slice. The good players all make a conscious effort to stay down over the ball and to reserve the use of the hands until the club is really in the hitting area.

In my observation, the other chief error most golfers make with a long iron is one that apparently stems from that frequently repeated instruction to take a shorter swing with a long iron than with a wood. Many players consequently take less than a full pivot on the backswing, and then make matters worse by trying to throw in some extra body action at contact. The first thing a player should remember is that the swing with the long iron is no different from the swing with the wood, except that, the shaft being shorter, the golfer must stand closer to the ball. Come back with a full backswing and a complete pivot, and when you move into the ball you will have all the power you need—and you will know it.

Correct: full backswing
and pivot

Incorrect: restricted
backswing and pivot

from **AL ESPOSITO**
Country Club of Charleston, S. C.

Pitching from Sandy Rough

O N SEASIDE and desert courses particularly but wherever sand exists, golfers run into a shot that few of them can cope with successfully. This is a short, lofted pitch from the sandy rough that must carry over a nearby embankment to reach the green. The object, obviously, is to get the ball up and over the embankment without punching it with so much forward drive that it either carries or rolls on over the green—where, of course, a nice little trap is usually lying in wait. In his consternation when he finds himself beset with this shot, the average golfer does little more than try to get the shot over with.

If the golfer will keep calm and regard this shot as a cousin of the explosion shot—which it primarily is—he will find he can deal with it without much trouble. Use your wedge, with your feet together and your hands a shade forward. Take the club back a little on the outside, with the left hand in charge. Hit the sand about an inch behind the ball. Don't let the hands roll over as you go through the ball. Keep the back of the left hand pointing up toward the sky on the follow-through. The ball should come up arching high and should fall without too much forward roll.

Play the lie in sandy rough as
an explosion shot

**TIP
FROM
THE
TOP**

from **JOHN THOREN**
*Myopia Hunt Club.
So. Hamilton, Mass*

Curing the Smothered Hook

A TIP that really seems to help my members is the one I use on the practice tee to cure players who are afflicted with quick or smothered hooks. The players who are vulnerable to the smothered hook are almost invariably very right-hand conscious. To drive home to them the proper use of the left hand, I get them to learn to take the right hand completely off the club as they enter the hitting area, which is approximately where the hands pass the right hip on the downstroke.

The practice tee is the place to do this. At first, many players find they can't release the right hand. After five or six tries, though, they can get the right hand off the club at the desired time and can swing through perfectly with only the left hand. This comes as a shock to them—they would never have thought it possible.

Hitting balls for a half-hour or so, using this right-hand release, gives the player a totally different concept of the golf swing. After he returns to hitting the ball with both hands, he no longer clutches the club in a death grip with his right hand, and he goes on to develop the correct feeling he's learned of hitting the ball with the back part of the left hand.

Hitting with left
hand only

Point of right-hand release

Hitting with both
hands

83

from **GARDNER DICKINSON, JR.**
Panama City, Fla.

Active Legwork

IF YOU are constructed like George Bayer—the last time I looked, George stood six-feet-five and weighed around 240—and if you are strong and well-coordinated to boot, whipping the club through the ball at a tremendous speed calls for no extraordinary measures. You simply swing and it happens. On the other hand, slim fellows of medium height like myself (who are outweighed almost two to one by the likes of George) really have to work at developing club-head speed.

Footwork is what will do it for the player of slim build, and that is what I give the balance of my practice time to—developing the action with my feet and legs that will make up for lack of brawn. On the backswing, in order to prevent any swaying and in order to store up maximum energy to release later, I push forward, to the inside, on the instep of my right foot. This helps you harness your power, but you must be sure you don't overdo it and tip forward with your trunk. Then, on the downswing, it helps me to increase my club-head acceleration, I find, if I push forward with my right knee—push it toward my left knee—as I am coming into the ball. Plenty of practice is required before this kind of footwork even begins to become second nature. But the added club-head speed produces added yardage that is more than worth all the hours you spend lowering the practice tees.

On backswing, Dickinson pushes forward on right instep

On downswing, Dickinson pushes forward with right knee

43	TIP FROM THE TOP

from **FAY CROCKER**
Club de Golf, Montevideo, Uruguay

Recovering Your Timing

WHEN I GET to forcing my shots, I am treading on dangerous ground: unless I catch myself immediately, I will get my swing completely out of timing. Getting it back is no easy matter.

The soundest method I know of to recover your timing is by swinging slower—all the way through the swing, I mean, from the waggle at address through the finish. Here's the way I look at it. A player generates club-head velocity—the factor behind distance—through the speed with which he, or she, can whip his hands through the ball. Fundamentally, this is a matter of strength but strength that is tempered by balance and rhythm and the accurate path of the club head—in short, the elements of control. High-handicap players snatch at the ball with a violent burst of energy, thinking they are increasing the speed of the club head. They're not. That snatching action is almost like starting the swing from scratch. It derives nothing at all from what has gone previously into the swing and delivers its power wrong, whereas pace and power are building all the way in a swing that is under control. When you lose your groove, you will save time and increase the life span of your wedge by slowing down every action. Then, once your timing has returned, you can gradually up the tempo of the coordinated swing you've rebuilt, and your timing will stay intact.

To recover timing, change tempo of swing
from too fast (left) to slow and even
(right)

44 TIP FROM THE TOP

from **BILL ZONKER**
Seattle Golf Club, Seatle, Wash.

Tapping the Putt

PUTTING to most non-golfers looks to be a very simple performance, but to most golfers it is a nerve-wracking test that varies in results from day to day. A favorite expression regarding a beginner who is enjoying good results on the green is that he "hasn't yet found out how difficult putting is." Putting is assuredly one department of golf where most players allow themselves to think too much about what they may do wrong, and this is what makes it so tough.

One positive approach to putting I would like to stress is this: First, be sure that you look at that "spot" on the ball which is directly behind the line to the hole. Try to imagine that a chalked line runs from the hole to that spot on the ball (allowing for the roll on this line, of course, when you do not have a straight putt). Then try to tap the ball crisply so that it will roll right on top of that chalked line to the hole.

Too much cannot be said about tapping the ball crisply. A lot of golfers have gotten off on the wrong track because putting has been explained to them as a stroke in which no precise contact is made with the ball. Trying to stroke the ball fluidly, they tend to stroke it over-gently. The result is they develop a push or pat stroke that has no conviction. Try tapping the putt. The ball must be hit smoothly, but it must be hit.

Try to imagine that a chalked line
runs from the ball to the hole

45	TIP FROM THE TOP

from JIMMY HINES
Thunderbird Country Club,
Palm Springs, Calif.

The Excessive Pivot

ONE OF THE WORST FAULTS in golf is not getting off your left foot on the backswing. An equally bad fault is getting too far off it. I find the best way to avoid either fault is to leave about twenty-five per cent of your weight on the inside ball of your left foot on the backswing, with the left heel just slightly off the ground. By concentrating on leaving a quarter of your weight on your left side, you do two services to your swing: (*1*) You insure that you get down solid on your left heel on the downswing. And (*2*) you insure that you don't take too much pivot.

Overpivoting is caused by the player's thinking that, if he really turns his back on the ball on the backswing, he will "wheel into it" on the downswing. This is exactly what he will do. He will twist so far away from the line of flight on the backswing that he will be obliged to twist equally far away from it on the downswing. An accurate hit becomes impossible.

As the diagram on the opposite page illustrates, not only does the player who overpivots and who pulls all of his weight off the left foot end up by doing an off-balance toe dance, but also the path of his club describes an arc that has a distorted relationship to the true line of flight.

90

The excessive pivot

Arc of club head in
overpivot swing

Arc of club head in
correct pivot swing

The correct pivot

46

TIP

FROM

THE

TOP

from **SAM SNEAD**
Greenbrier Country Club,
White Sulphur Springs, W. Va.

Chipping from the Fringe

THE SCORING in golf, as everyone knows, is done around the greens. Even our finest golfers don't hit all the greens— a number of our top-circuit scorers miss quite a few—but they can get down in two from off the edge just like clockwork. Some over-90-shooters I've played with score that low only because they're pretty proey around the green, but the average over-90-shooter loses many saveable strokes because he doesn't understand how to play a chip. This is one so-called simple shot that is really a simple shot. The average player, though, thinks he has to pitch the ball up in the air. He uses too lofted a club. He overpivots—transfers his weight too much—and swings so fast he can't get his weight back to the ball quick enough. As a result, he looks up, he fluffs, he scalps, he does everything.

Treat the chip from the fringe as a long putt. From a foot off the edge to fifteen or so feet off, don't take too lofted a club. Stand with your feet close together. Get your weight a bit on your left side and keep it there. Forget about lofting the ball, and play a brief, crisp little running stroke, relying on your sense of distance to tell you how hard to hit the shot, just as you would on a long approach putt.

The feet are close together, the weight slightly on left side, on the chip from the fringe

47

TIP FROM THE TOP

from **BEVERLY HANSON**
Apple Valley, Calif.

Flexing the Knees

WHENEVER they attend a tournament to watch the top pros or amateurs in action, it is the serious intention of most golfers to study the stars' technique and thereby improve their own. This is easier said than done, for most golfers find that, when they watch a top player, they become so intrigued with the player's personality and so absorbed by the flight of the ball that it is next to impossible to concentrate on the niceties of technique.

I mention this because, if you studied the stars attentively, you would observe that the one fundamental that almost every fine technician puts into practice is the comfortable flexing of the knees. When you assume your stance, the knees should break forward comfortably, and the same amount of flex should be maintained throughout the swing. Women players particularly are prone to lock their legs stiffly at address. All fluid motion is then denied them, and the best they can do is to brace themselves backwards on a locked right leg and then jump off the right side to the left side. This can be easily avoided by swinging with your knees relaxed and flexible—just as you would do for ballroom dancing. This permits ease of movement and flow of motion.

Incorrect: knees stiff

Correct: knees flexed

48 | TIP
FROM
THE
TOP

from **PALMER MAPLES**
Benvenue Country Club,
Rocky Mount, N. C.

The Pause at the Top

A DISTINGUISHING FEATURE of the swings of top-notch golfers —so goes one of the clichés of the locker room—is the definite pause between the completion of the backswing and the beginning of the downswing. Some clarification of this point would, I think, be helpful. The impression most golfers get when they watch a fine player is that all movement ceases during the pause he makes at the top of his swing. It does look that way to the untrained eye, but in reality the frozen pause, as such, doesn't exist. It is the effect produced when the wrists begin to flex back (in a counter-clockwise arc) as they reverse their direction and begin the downswing.

The average golfer who wants to get the feeling of this so-called pause can do so if he times his swing by saying to himself, "Swing back and through." The "and" would then coincide with that period of the swing in which his hands hold the club at the top of his backswing while the wrists reverse into the downswing. There is more than just good looks to this action, as there is in all good style. It is a refinement of timing that inevitably leads to the proper extension of the wrists and arms at contact. Although this apparent pause is present in the good golf swing, it is never present in the stiff and tense golf swing. What makes for the pausing effect is leaving out all effort to achieve it.

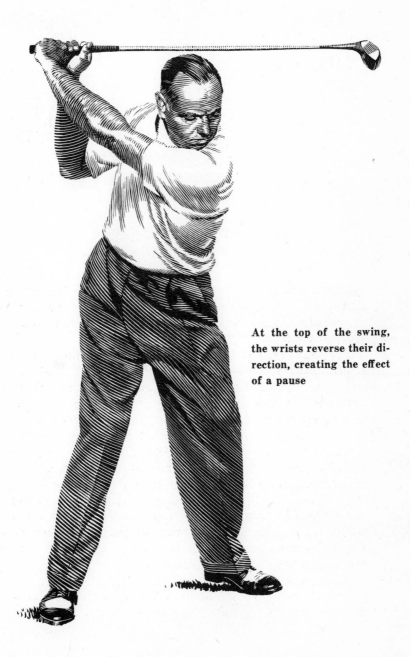

At the top of the swing, the wrists reverse their direction, creating the effect of a pause

TIP
FROM
THE
TOP

from **CHARLES McKENNA**
Oak Hill Country Club,
Rochester, N. Y.

The Foundation of Rhythm

ANY AVERAGE GOLFER who wants to play a better game must have a good basic foundation on which to work. I mean, of course, a proper pivot. Here's a way to acquire that fundamental action.

Take a club like a five-iron and start sweeping it into a backswing as naturally as you can, but swing back only until the left arm is parallel with the ground. Let your left foot rise normally and roll against its right sole edge. Let your left knee bend easily towards a point midway between your two feet. Your swing has thus traveled only halfway to the top of a full backswing. Then swing the club forward, reversing the action so that your right foot rolls onto its left sole edge, the heel raising slightly. The weight of your body will shift onto the left leg and foot. Try to keep this footwork in time with the swing of the club. In a very short time you will sense a feeling of rhythm. If you will practice this short rhythmic swing ten minutes a day for two weeks, you'll be surprised at the feeling of coordination you get.

Now you can begin swinging at a ball. Don't try to knock the cover off. The rhythmic action of your feet, knees, and hips will produce the swinging power themselves.

The player with a correct basic
pivot finds that his right side, the
power side, moves gracefully into
his swing

from **GRAHAM ROSS**
Dallas Athletic Club Country Club,
Dallas, Texas

The Movement of the Right Arm

PROBABLY no single movement in the golf swing has more to do with controlled power than the movement and position of the upper right arm. The short arc the arm moves through as it nears the top of the backswing and then begins the downswing can be likened to the wing motion of a bird. It lifts up and away from the side at the top of the backswing, then settles back and against the side as the club proceeds through its downward arc.

It is not a tense motion. The right arm is not pressed against the side. But the upper right arm must return to a snug position against the side and remain there until the club head has moved through the ball. By being anchored there, it serves as a fulcrum around which the right forearm moves, thus providing the hitting power of the swing. Moreover, if the arm is returned naturally to the side as the body turns in the downswing, the golfer will be in balance through the hitting area.

It is the upper arm that starts the downward arc, until it rests easily against the right side. Then the right forearm continues the arc of the swing until the club head is through the ball.

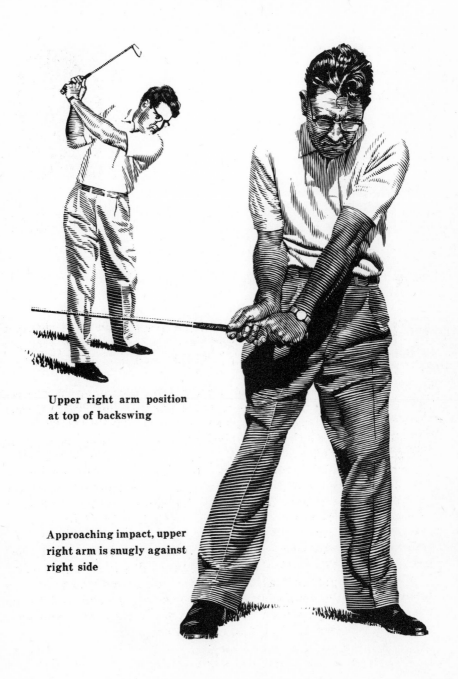

Upper right arm position at top of backswing

Approaching impact, upper right arm is snugly against right side

51

TIP

FROM

THE

TOP

from **WILLIE KLEIN**
La Gorce Country Club,
Miami Beach, Fla.

The Line to the Target

I LIKE TO IMAGINE that a railroad track runs from the spot where I'm standing right up to the green. My feet are planted squarely on one rail of the track and the ball is positioned on the other track.

If this sounds like a foolish method for setting up your direction, consider the square-your-shoulders-to-the-target method many golfers use. By squaring his shoulders to the flag, say, the golfer feels that he will be hitting on a straight line towards the flag. That feeling is deceiving, however. Unless the golfer automatically compensates—and a lot of golfers do this—chances are the ball will go sailing off to the right of center, for there is a tendency to cut across the ball in an effort to keep it square on the object. The club closes in instead of hitting from the inside out.

After a few swings the railroad-track method begins to feel natural. The tracks of the imaginary railroad come to a point at the target, just as the tracks of a real railroad appear to merge in the distance. On the downswing the club will feel as if it's going to whack the ball far to the right of that target point. It won't. You'll be right on line.

52

**TIP
FROM
THE
TOP**

from **BABE ZAHARIAS**

The Enjoyment of Golf

GOLF IS ALWAYS for pleasure. A great many people who play it are apt to forget that. Their forgetfulness is understandable, because there never was a game that could compare with golf's amazing ability to make a person search for lower and lower scores and for perfection in shotmaking. The average golfer's desire to improve his or her game is certainly laudable, as long as the golfer keeps a sense of proportion. A weekend golfer whose business is not golf should not go at the game as though it were work. People who make their living at golf must necessarily give it all they have, but people for whom it is a recreation should treat it as a recreation.

This is not to say that some application is not necessary or desirable for even the weekend golfer. I think it is a darn good idea for every golfer to attempt to play the game as well as his or her natural talents allow. With this in mind you must make provision to do some practicing, to approach your shots seriously, to try to get around in the lowest number of strokes, and to outplay your opponent in a match. All this is fine, as long as you approach your goals in golf with the proper spirit and do not try to attain unattainable goals. If you do, you are denying yourself the basic reward of this wonderful game, which is the rare enjoyment it provides.